Edward

Yen Yuen

A Noisy Noise Annoys

This book is dedicated to LAURA CURRY

whose noise is my delight

A Noisy Noise Annoys

COMPILED BY
JENNIFER CURRY

Illustrated by
SUSIE JENKIN-PEARCE

RED FOX

A Red Fox Book

Published by Random House Children's Books
20 Vauxhall Bridge Road, London SW1V 2SA

A division of Random House UK Ltd
London Melbourne Sydney Auckland
Johannesburg and agencies throughout the world

1 3 5 7 9 10 8 6 4 2

First published simultaneously in hardback and paperback by
The Bodley Head Children's Books and Red Fox 1996

Printed and bound in Great Britain by
Cox & Wyman Ltd, Reading, Berkshire

Papers used by Random House UK Ltd are natural, recyclable products made
from wood grown in sustainable forests. The manufacturing processes conform
to the environmental regulations of the country of origin.

RANDOM HOUSE UK Limited Reg. No. 954009

ISBN 0 09 952801 0

CONTENTS

DOZE FOR FIVE MINUTES MORE

A Poem to be Spoken Silently

It was so silent that I heard
my thoughts rustle
like leaves in a paper bag ...

It was so silent that I heard
the trees ease off
their coats of bark ...

It was so still that I felt
a raindrop's grin
as it tickled the window pane ...

It was so silent that I heard
a page in this book
whisper to its neighbour,
'Look, he's peering at us again ...'

It was so silent that I sensed
a smile crack the face
of a stranger ...

It was so silent that I heard
the morning earth roll over
in its sleep and doze
for five minutes more ...

Pie Corbett

Daybreak

This morning I heard dawn breaking
Shattering the dark into day
And night exploded into light
As the silence slipped away.

Janis Priestley

A Crack Band

Early morning boiler gives a bagpipe bellow,
starts to heat the water, makes it chuckle like
a cello,

radiators wake up with a tinging and a ping –
pizzicato plucking of a violin,

metal's making music on a xylophone,
pipes are groaning notes like an old
trombone,

castanets are clacking, there's a clanging from
a gong
as the house warms up and the band plays on.

Gina Douthwaite

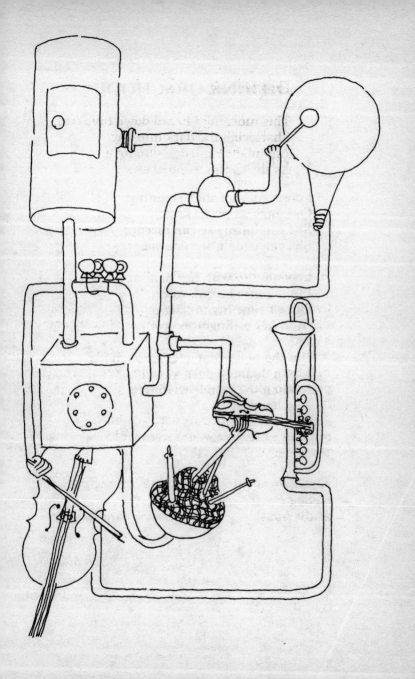

I THINK OF SCHOOL

In Class

I don't mind if she's shouting,
Or bangs on piano keys;
She can hum; she can hiccup;
She can cough; she can sneeze.

I can put up with her reading
In the same boring voice;
Out-of-tune hymn-singing
(And her yelling 'Rejoice!')

But the noise that goes through me
Like a double-edged sword
Is when she stands writing;
And her nails
       S
          C
            R
              A
                P
                  E
                      the board.

Robert Sparrow

Sounds

Miss asked if we had any favourite sounds,
and could we quickly write them down.
Tim said the *screeeeam* of a mean guitar
or a saxophone or a fast sports car.
Shakira said cats when they *purr* on your lap,
and Jamie, the CRASH of a thunderclap.
Paul asked what word he could possibly write
for the sound of a rocket on Guy Fawkes
Night,
or a redwood tree as it fell to the ground
and Miss said to write it as it sounds.
So Paul wrote *Whoooooooooooosh* with a
dozen o's
and CRACK with a crack in it, just to show
the kind of noise a tree might make
as it hit the ground *and* made it SHAKE".
Then everyone began to call, hey listen to this,
what do you think? Or is this right Miss,
I can't decide, if balloons go POP or BANG
or BUST, *and* do bells peeeal or just CLANG?
Then Miss said it was quite enough
and time to stop all the silly stuff.
What she really likes, as she's often said
is a quiet room, with every head
bent over books, writing things down.
The sound of silence, her favourite sound!

Brian Moses

Chemistry Lesson

Bubble, fizz,
Whiz and bang –
A Cauldron full
Of marbled sound.
Feet are shuffling,
Paper ruffling,
Stool legs scraping.
Doors are slamming.
Listen to the
Coughing, choking,
Clinking, clanking,
Test tubes boiling,
Bunsens burning.
Sparks are spraying,
Rising, falling,
Landing in a glow of red.
Listen to the
Murmurs gurgling,
Whispers growing,
Voices rising.
'Silence!'
Concentration,
Eyes are watching,
All ears listening.
Pens at paper
Heads bent low,
Brains in action,
Churning, turning,
All are working.

Elizabeth Ingate (12)

I Hear . . .

When I think of school
I hear
High shouts tossed
Like juggled balls in windy yards, and lost
In gutters, treetops, air.
And always, somewhere,
Piano-notes water-fall
And small sharp voices wail.
A monster-roar surges – 'Goal!'
The bell.
Then doors slam. There's the kick, scruff,
stamp of shoes
Down corridors that trap and trail echoes.
Desk-tops thud with books, kit-bags,
A child's ghost screams as her chair's pushed
back.
Laughter bubbles up and bursts.
Screech-owl whistles. Quick-fox quarrel-flares.
The voice barks 'QUIET!'
All sit. All wait.
Till scraped chalk shrieks
And whispers creep.
Cough. Ruler crack. Desk creak.
And furtive into the silence comes
A tiny mouse-scrabbling of pens.
Scamper. Stop. Scamper. Stop. Tiptoe.
And there, just outside the top window
As if it had never ceased to be
But only needed listening to
A scatter of birdsong, floating free.

Berlie Doherty

Bird (Play) Time

Children shouting, hollering, screaming
Playtime
Crisp packet whirls, crumbs flying
Playtime
Whistle blows, shouts stop, feet shuffle
Playtime
Wind whips the playground debris
Playtime

Loud squawking and whirring wings
Birdtime
Clearing the crummy surface.

Karlen Lawrence

MUSIC TWISTS AROUND MY EARS

Music

```
                        k
             l          c
             e          i
             s          t
             p          s
          a
        e  r
      y    i
      m    c
      d    k
      n    l   M  u   i c
      u    e      s
      o        d      t w
      r    a   i   s i
               s
      s        a
        r   e  p
            a  p
               e
```

David Poulter

20

Concerts

Half my life ago
When I was six years old
I delighted in a teacher.
She taught me to play the tin whistle.
The sound of the Irish hills
Where we lived
Flowed from this thin, reedy, golden pipe.
At her final concert,
Standing in my best yellow frock
And home knitted jumper,
My photograph was taken
Piping a sad farewell.
Now in England
I play a recorder.
The sound feels more restrained,
Though the tunes are lively, joyful and
happy.
I perform
In an orchestra.
I wear formal clothes.
The music exhilarates me,
Even though nostalgia
For my golden pipe
May knock at my door.

Oka Russell (12)

The Concert

The Drums went bang
The Cymbals clashed
The Cello plucked nervously
And frightened the Flute
Playing like a mouse
Scampering around the floor
Violins creaked like doors
While we sat
In a patchwork of schools
Shuddering
And waiting for our turn.

Simon Laslett (8)

Improved Reception

No nerve was left unjangled
When Nicola learnt the fiddle.
She scraped it high
She scraped it low
She scraped it in the middle.
As soon as she was quite awake
Our eardrums all began to ache:
I knew I'd made a big mistake
To let her learn the fiddle.

Relentlessly she tortured us,
She practised all she could;
And then one day I noticed
She was getting pretty good.
No longer were we suffering
Cacophonous vibrations,
Instead our ears were treated
To more tuneful presentations.

And so, I've stopped complaining
About the dreadful din;
I proudly say to all my friends,
'*My* daughter plays the violin.'

Mike Jubb

Heavy Metal

Tension is building.
Can you feel it?
You can never be prepared,
No matter how you try.
The guitar howls and screams,
And a drummer fights his kit.
The volume builds up,
And it flows to a crescendo.
You can feel the energy from beneath.
Bursting from the ground,
And spiralling up your legs,
It makes you want to run,
It makes you want to shout,
It makes you want to tear down the walls
That stop you getting out.

Marcus Knight (14)

Fragment

My father lifted
a mouth-organ up
to the wind on a hill

and the wind of Bohemia
sighed a few
frail and blue notes

man and child
in a harebell light
frail ghosts . . . faint tune

Gerda Mayer

The Little Dancers

Lonely, save for a few faint stars, the sky
Dreams; and lonely, below, the little street
Into its gloom retires, secluded and shy.
Scarcely the dumb roar enters this soft
retreat;
And all is dark, save where come flooding
rays
From a tavern window: there, to the brisk
measure
Of an organ that down in an alley merrily
plays,
Two children, all alone and no one by,
Holding their tattered frocks, through an airy
maze
Of motion, lightly threaded with nimble feet,
Dance sedately: face to face they gaze,
Their eyes shining, grave with a perfect
pleasure.

Laurence Binyon

There Were These Two Girls

there were these two girls
strutting down the street
whistling
loud enough to crack the windows

they were whistling
at the moon
but the moon just winked
as it hid behind a cloud

they were whistling
at the lamp-posts
but the lamp-posts just blinked
as they leaned together
like drunks

they were whistling
at the boys
who slinked off round the corner
like shamefaced puppies
with their tails between their legs

they were whistling
at the world
then they stood there listening
to see
if the world would whistle back

Dave Ward

Two Tooters

A tutor who tooted the flute
Tried to tutor two tooters to toot.
   Said the two to the tutor,
    'Is it harder to toot, or
To tutor two tooters to toot?'

Anon

Singing

The children are singing,
their mouths open like sleepy fish.
Our teacher conducting the class
waves her arms
like a rhyme in water.
The girls sing high:
our ears ring for the sweetness.
Listeners stand in dazzling amazement.

Peter Sheton (10)

Telephone Wires

Jacqueline Brown

from The Tempest – The Isle is Full of Noises

The isle is full of noises,
Sounds, and sweet airs, that give delight and
hurt not.
Sometimes a thousand twangling instruments
Will hum about mine ears; and sometimes
voices,
That, if I then had waked after long sleep,
Will make me sleep again.

William Shakespeare

IT ROARS. I RIDE

Fast Rider

We are one.
We bend together
leather legs
bent arms bent handle bars
bent fingers rigid
revving up for bends.

It roars. I ride.

I am a bullet
stretching air
to rocket through.
Hard skull with eyes
and nose, lips, tongue and teeth
inside.

It roars. I ride.

I need thighs
and knees to grip
the power I own.
All this is mine
behind, between, beyond.
I'm coming
fast, astride.

It roars. I ride.

Jane Whittle

Underground Train

It roars through the tunnel,
A monster growling and rushing,
Its hot breath blows out,
Lifting my skirt
And it's a fight to hold it down.
Lights beam out like shining eyes,
It squeals to a halt,
Its doors open wide and swallow me up.

Ellen Coffey (7)

The Cars That Leave Our Street

The cars that leave our street
start up in different ways.
Some cough and splutter, then jerk into life,
some tremble and shake, jump forward
then brake, some moan as if
they have belly ache, some shudder and
rumble,
some bellow or grumble, some ROAR
with a burst of fire power, some shiver
and cower. Some creep along
as if something's wrong, some leap
with a spurt of speed, some need
the magic touch, the press of a button,
flick of a switch. Some purr along
without a hitch, smooth operators,
shiny and smug, some stubbornly refuse
to break into a chug. Some are well-
mannered,
quietly spoken, but one old car,
the one that's mine, despite kicking,
pleading, coaxing, just can't be woken!

Brian Moses

Rickety Train Ride

I'm taking the train to Ricketywick.
Clickety clickety clack.
I'm sat in my seat
with a sandwich to eat
as I travel the trickety track.

It's an ever so rickety trickety train,
and I honestly thickety think
that before it arrives
at the end of the line
it will tip up my drippety drink.

Tony Mitton

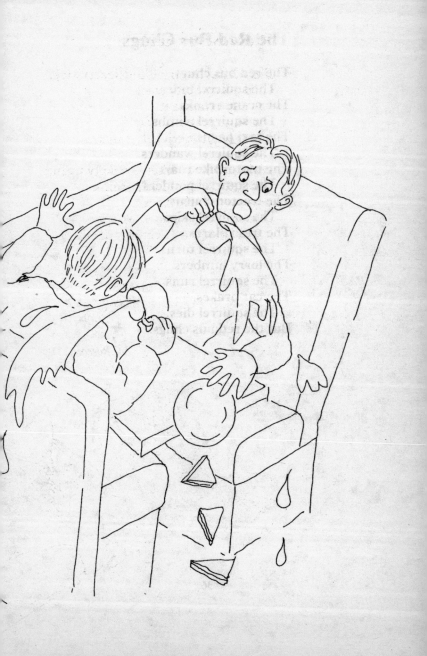

The Red Bus Chugs

The red bus chugs.
   The squirrel hides.
The crane cranks.
   The squirrel climbs.
The taxi parps.
   The squirrel wanders.
The motorbike roars.
   The squirrel ponders.
The tractor churns.
   The squirrel skips.
The train blares.
   The squirrel turns.
The lorry lumbers.
   The squirrel runs.
The car brakes.
   The squirrel dies.
But the red bus chugs.

Zoe Roscoe (13)

Low Flying

Under my knees damp ground
is soft, easy to weed.
One by one, out they come
and the earth lies there in the sound
of a warm afternoon. Bees feed
in the ivy, seeped in a feathery hum.

The stream chuckles in stone holes
smoothing big rocks where the worms
hide.
Small sounds creep into silence
spreading like oil on a pool . . .

but then . . . the whole sky unrolls
and splits in my skull; air shrieks aside
leaving a buzz in the bones – the sense
of a sound so loud it could tear out

the roots of great trees,
rip feathers from wings, or flatten a cow.
Vibrating like plucked wire,
unable to breathe, I cling to my clamped
knees.
Too fast to be seen, the plane made a row
that hurt in my head for an hour.

Jane Whittle

CRUNKLE, CRUNCH, SLURP

Sort Of (Crunkle Crunch Slurp)

My brother always tries
to tell stories at breakfast.
They are usually very complicated
and we get lost in the first sentence.

'It was like this you see,'
(munch, crunch, slurp)
'this man,' (munch, crunch, slurp)
'lived in a castle and
there was this other man,'
(munch, crunch) 'who lived
in another sort of castle altogether.'

By this time my brother is into the toast
and spreading it badly all over the place,

'and the first man, you see,
sort of,' (crackle, crunch, drop) 'eurgh!
didn't like the other man, who lived,'
(wipe, wipe, smear) 'well, it wasn't actually
in a sort of castle, more of a,'
(crunkle, crunch)
'Oh I've got marmite all over my track suit!'

Mum says, 'I told you you would.'

'And the first man got into a sort of helicopter,
though it wasn't really a . . .'

By this time he is talking to himself.
Everyone else has disappeared,
to the loo, or cleaning their teeth.

'helicopter, it was a really weird,'
(crunkle, crunch, slurp).

David Scott

Cousin Janice with the Big Voice

When my cousin Janice
Opens her mouth to speak
A storm kindles behind her teeth
And a gale pours out.
This is a voice used
To holding conversations
With cows and sheep and dogs
Across mountains and valleys.
But here across the table-cloth
In our small flat
When she asks for the sugar
The tea cups tremble
And a tidal wave foments
In the eddies of the cherry trifle.

Gareth Owen

40

The Night Dad Turned 40!

Hubub, hubub, hubub, hubub
Hubububub, hubububub
Hubububububububub,
Hubub, hubub, hubub, glug.
Glug, glug, hubub, glug glug-
Glugluglugluglugluglug,
Ahhhhhhhhhh.
Tch-tch-boom-
Sp-tch-tch boom.
Tch-tch-boom-
Sp-tch-tch boom.
Tapity-tapity-tapity-tapity
Tch-tch-boom-
Sp-tch-tch-
Tapity-tapity-tapity-glug.
Tch-tch-boom-
Sp-tch-tch glug,
Glug, glug, hubbub, glug
Tapity-tapity . . . tapity . . . tapity
Hruk, hruk, hruk hru . . .urrrrrrrrrrrrgh.
Hruuuurghhhh.
 (splatter)!
Rhubarb, rhubarb, rhubarb, rhubarb
Rhubub, hubub, hubub, hubub,
Hubub . . . hub
Bub. . . . bub.
. . . Hub.
ZZZZZZZZZZZZZZZZZZ!

David Thake Stallibrass (15)

42

It was Just as I Knew . . .

It was just as I knew it would be,
I sat next to the Duchess at tea.
The noises abdominal
Were something phenomenal –
And everyone thought it was ME!

Anon

43

In the Kitchen

In the kitchen
After the aimless
Chatter of the plates,
The murmuring of the gas,
The chuckles of the water pipes
And the sharp exchanges
Of the knives, forks and spoons,
Comes the serious quiet
When the sink slowly clears its throat,
And you can hear the occasional rumble
Of the refrigerator's tummy
As it digests the cold.

John Cotton

Burp

Pardon me
for being so rude.
It was not me
it was my food.
It just came up
to say hallo.
Now it's gone
back down below.

Anon

OWLS HOOT, BEARS SNORE

The Reason Why

The reason why
the fly
annoys me,
as it does,
is that,
however hard I try,
I can't ignore its buzz

Tony Mitton

Unrattled

Two rattling magpies
machine-gun their anger
from a branch
in the horse chestnut.

Passing under the tree
the cause of this clackety-racket
pauses, yawns,
twitches a contemptuous tail
then pads silently on,
pretending not to notice.

Mike Jubb

The Howl

Rarely – on one or two nights a year –
a lingering, wonderful wolf-howl
escapes from the mouth of our
sleeping dog
fills the slumbering house
floats over the darkened town –
a globe of longing, a sphere of dream
where black forests spike an icy sky
in silvered landscapes, and grey shapes
slip silently
from lairs of shadow.

Margaret Banthorpe

Manor House at Dusk

The peacock brays
Like a cold siren.
Its cry hangs menacing
Over turret, fountain, urn.
At dusk its banshee wail
Shadows our covered walk.
Footsteps quicken. We turn,
Haunted by waterfall eyes.

Daphne Schiller

Frogs in Water

There was a splash when the frogs
Jumped in the water.
   A ripple,
   A wobble,
   A stir.
They are deaf to the songbirds
   but
When the rain comes down
And pats the water as if it were a dog,
The frogs gently listen.

Andrew Abbott (10)

The Whale's Hymn

In an ocean before cold dawn broke
Covered by an overcoat
I lay awake in a boat
And heard a whale.

Hearing a song so solemn and so calm
It seemed absurd to feel alarm –
But I had a notion it sang
God's favourite hymn,

And spoke direct to Him.

Brian Patten

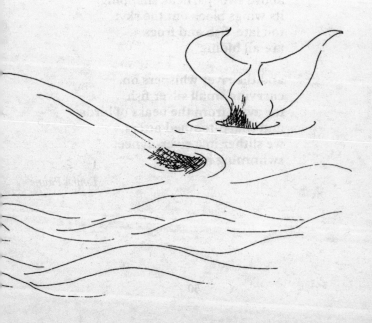

A Quiet Life

We are a family
of fish,
we shimmer under the water,
touch it and
flash
we are gone

a quiet life we have,
we hear only bubbles
bursting on the surface,
tadpoles wriggling their tails,
little frogs jumping

a thrill of danger when a bird
above swoops, beak snapping,
its wings block out the sky:
too late, fish and frogs
are all hiding

and the river whispers on,
carrying small silver fish
far away from the beaks of birds
and sharp-toothed otters,
we slither in a river-dance,
swimming in time

Emma Payne

I Speak I Say I Talk

Cats purr Lions roar
Owls hoot Bears snore
Crickets creak Mice squeak
Sheep baa But I *speak!*

Monkeys chatter Cows moo
Ducks squawk Doves coo
Pigs squeal Horses neigh
Chickens cluck But I *say!*

Flies hum Dogs growl
Bats screech Coyotes howl
Frogs croak Parrots squawk
Bees buzz But I *talk!*

Colum Deery (8)

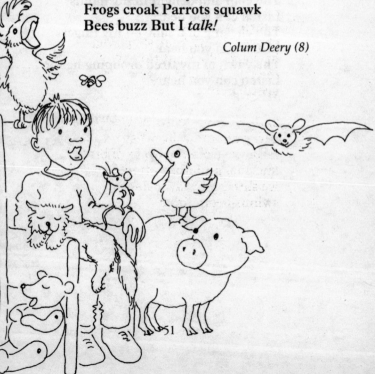

51

CAN YOU HEAR ME?

Body Sounds

Listen can you hear
The thud and echo of my heart?
Listen can you hear
The rumble of my empty stomach?
Listen can you hear
The trickling of my warm blood?
Listen can you hear
The clap and delight in my hands?
Listen can you hear
The clicking of a tune on my fingers?
Listen can you hear
The yawn of my tired drooping head?
Listen can you hear
ME!

Lauren Julian (8)

Talk

I wish people, when you sit near them,
Wouldn't think it necessary to make
conversation
And send their draughts of words
Blowing down your neck and your ears
And giving you a cold in your inside.

D. H. Lawrence

The Sound of Silence

Birdsong shrill,
Birdsong sweet,
Horse clip-clopping
Down the street

Revving engine,
Old church bell,
Fire alarm,
Waved sea-shell.

Father's snoring,
Mother's sigh,
Brother sneezing
Baby's cry.

Lowing cattle,
Barking dog,
Bleating lamb,
Croaking frog.

Beating hammer,
Tick of clock,
Clicking needles,
Key in lock.

Singing choir,
Creaking floor,
Fat in chip-pan,
Scratching paw.

Shouts of children,
Echo wall.
But the old deaf man –
Hears no sound at all.

John Kitching

My Mum

My mum's a chatterbox.
Her real name is Constance.
But everyone calls her Connie.
When she gets talking,
There's no stopping her.

Before she married,
Her name was Walker.
So her schoolteacher
Nicknamed her Constant Talker!

My mum's a livewire.
She's full of fun.
She's always laughing and joking.
When she gets the giggles,
There's no stopping her.

Her married name
Is Constance Wrigley.
So the neighbours have
Nicknamed her Constant Giggly!

John Foster

Having My Ears Done

People's voices were wrapped in cotton
wool.
My own rattled in a closed tunnel.
'See Nurse,' said the Doctor.

She pumped water in my ears
Pulsing like an outboard motor.
It ran out with a crackle.

The world came alive and imploded.
'OK?' said Nurse. 'Don't shout,' I said.
'My normal voice,' she answered.

In the waiting room,
Opened newspapers cracked like thunder.
Footsteps on the floor were bells ringing.

My anorak spat out electric sparks.
And jeans hissed together.
Shoes creaked like old doors.

Outside, birds chirping their heads off
Were steel chisels striking stone.
I could even hear the grass grow.

Robert Sparrow

Lides to Bary Jade
(Mary Jane)

The bood is beabig brighdly love,
The sdars are shidig too;
While I ab gazig dreabily
Add thigkig, love, of you;
You caddot, oh, you caddot kdow,
By darlig, how I biss you –
(Oh, whadt a fearful cold I've got –
Ck-*tish*-u! Ck-ck-*tish*-u!)

Anon

The Sound of Tears

I feel I can hear them –
your tears slipping
from the corners of your eyes.
They fall, clockwork,
marking time,
making time –
a sad time.
Listen now.
You can hear too –
My child crying.

'Come dry your face –
dry your face
in the wishing wind.'

Tim Pointon

Children in the Park

ROAR!
   Come the voices through the woods,
   Rattling the trees and the ground;
   An onslaught of paws and claws
   Pushes its way through the leaves
   And into the clearing.
   The lion pounces on a rock. Then . . .

WHOOSH!
   The waves lap up
   Against the island;
   The ship-wrecked girls
   Sprawl on the beach.
   The rays from the sun
   Spray down on them. Then . . .

DING-A-LING!
   Goes the ice-cream van.
   'Come; I want a lolly,'
   Says the largest lion, and the
   Ship-wrecked girl races
   For some money from Mum.

Emma Ripper (15)

Noises Off

Ever been kissed by a toothless vampire?
  (gwaaalll-smacktup)
Ever thrown water on a Brownies' campfire?
  (splutsch-frisskress-kik)

Ever caught your socks on a rusty wire?
  (pir-keressfrick-twick)
Ever found and rolled an old car tyre?
  (coom-coom-roooo-rooo-roo-roodth)

Ever jumped in a barrel for a cooling drink?
  (whee-sklundftlslansh-blurburb-drok)
Ever bathed a baby in the kitchen sink?
  (splumge-splumge-thwogt-bunk-dribbledub)

Ever smashed a clock with a heavy hammer?
  (whoo-powcrunchaduncklecrash-tinkle-bink-ink-k)
Ever heard a barn owl stutter and stammer?
  (t-t-tw-twhit-twhit-t-t-twh-twhoo-hoo)

John Rice

Noisy (and Quiet) Places

In York
they squawk.
In Leek
they shriek.
In Dore
they roar.
On Skye
they cry.
But in Llanffairgwyn-thisperandthistle
they just, er,
whisper and whistle.

In Stoke
they croak.
In Fleet
they bleat.
In Diss
they hiss.
In Sale
they wail.
But in Llanffairgwyn-stumbleandstutter
they just, er,
mumble and mutter.

In Tring
    they sing.
In Stone
    they moan.
In Birse
    they curse.
In Stroud
    they're loud.
But in Llanffairgwyn-gruffleandgriffle
    they just, er,
      snuffle and sniffle.

Wes Magee

STARS CLICKING INTO PLACE

The Snow Monster

When the Snow Monster sneezes,
Flurries of snow swirl and whirl,
Twisting round trees, curling into crevices,
Brushing the ground a brilliant white.

When the Snow Monster bellows,
Blizzards blot out the sky,
Piling up drifts, blocking roads,
Burying the landscape in a white grave.

When the Snow Monster cries,
Soft flakes slip and slide gently down
Into the hands of waiting children
Who test their taste with their tongues.

When the Snow Monster sleeps,
The air crackles with children's laughter
As they throw snowballs, build snowmen
And whizz downhill on their sledges.

John Foster

from **A January Night**

The rain smites more and more
The east wind snarls and sneezes
Through the joints of the quivering door
The water wheezes.

Thomas Hardy

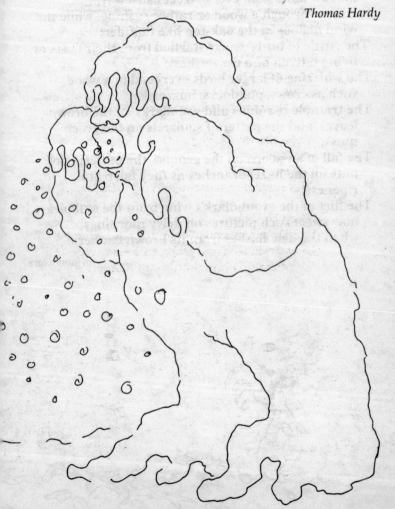

Pleasant Sounds

The rustling of leaves under the feet in woods and
   under hedges;
The crumping of cat-ice and snow down wood-rides,
   narrow lanes, and every street causeway;
Rustling through a wood or rather rushing, while the
   wind halloos in the oak-top like thunder;
The rustle of birds' wings startled from their nests or
   flying unseen into the bushes;
The whizzing of larger birds overhead in a wood,
   such as crows, puddocks, buzzards;
The trample of robins and woodlarks on the brown
   leaves, and the patter of squirrels on the green
   moss;
The fall of an acorn on the ground, the pattering of
   nuts on the hazel branches as they fall from
   ripeness;
The flirt of the groundlark's wing from the stubbles –
   how sweet such pictures on dewy mornings,
   when the dew flashes from its brown feathers!

John Clare

Rainstorm

A single drop
plop, plop, plop
joining other drops plop, plop, plop
plopplopplopplopplopplopplop
into rivers, on to crops,
getting thicker, louder, quicker
in the cities, on the streets
water coming down in sheets
raindrops dropping, never stopping
ad infinitum
plop, plop plopping

Katherine Gallagher

Seasons of the Wind – Four Haiku

Spring
March winds rage and roar.
Then their bullyboy bellow
sidles into Spring.

Jennifer Curry

Summer
The wind's fingertips
tickle the wave's bare tummy.
The seaside chortles.

Pie Corbett

Autumn
In ballet skirts of
red and gold, falling leaves dance
to the Autumn wind.

Jenny Craig

Winter
The angry gale writhes
and lashes its lion's tail.
Winter stalks the land.

Jenni Sinclair

Listen

Silence is when you can hear things.
Listen:
The breathing of bees,
A moth's footfall,
Or the mist easing its way
Across the field,
The light shifting at dawn
Or the stars clicking into place
At evening.

John Cotton

THE NIGHT SHAKES ME AWAKE

Sounds Like

In my room
I'm reading.
Eyes sucking at words
as though they are favourite sweets
until I'm lost inside my book world.

Some twenty pages later,
to rest my eyes
and test my ears
I play the listening game.

Downstairs Mum's voice is happily singing,
accompanied by water chuckling into the
  kitchen sink
and soon plates, dishes and cups
are setting sail across a bowl of bubbled foam.

Suddenly my baby sister
is pretending to be a police siren.
MUM-MEE! MUM-MEE! MUM-MEE!
MUM-MEE!
but her voice quickly screeches to a halt
as she spots a new target,
DOG-GEE! DOG-GEE! DOG-GEE!
DOG-GEE!

Meanwhile in the front room
all alone,
the television chats excitedly to itself
as it waits for an audience to arrive.

Some time later,
the house has yawned
and slowly drifted off to sleep.
Everything is
silent,
still,
frozen,
apart from the lick-tick of my bedroom clock,
not hurrying
just taking its time.

Ian Souter

Trying to Sleep

I cannot sleep
with all this racket –
you lot had better
pack it in.

But the wind wolf whistles
at the trees,
who shake their skirts
and flirt
with the breeze,
teasing and tossing
their hair,
while the bushes wheeze
and sneeze,
knocking their knees
like old men,
and the dustbins rattle
their sides
and clap their hands
from their grandstand view.
But – the houses stare
and bare their teeth.

The night shakes me
awake –
its sounds
surround us.

Pie Corbett

Birdsong Lullaby

As evening comes and blue light tints the
sky
sleepily I listen for the birdsong lullaby.
Waiting by my window I feel the cool
twilight,
hear the fidgeting of insects
who love to dance at night.
Then begins the singing, especially for me.
One bird's little solo becomes a choir tree.
'Chirr-up!', 'Chirr-up!', 'Cheer up!',
they seem to say.
Put drowsy head on pillow
while we sing the day away.

Pauline Stewart

Your Snores

Your snores
are such resounding snores,
such long, such loud,
astounding snores,
the sort of snores
that shake the doors,
that break the windows,
rattle the floors,
enduring snores,
deplorable snores,
such sore, such raw,
incurable snores,
such 'Roll on morning chorus' snores,
the sort of snore
you can't ignore,
snores that make you call, 'No more!
   – for goodness' sake,
      wake up!'

Celia Warren

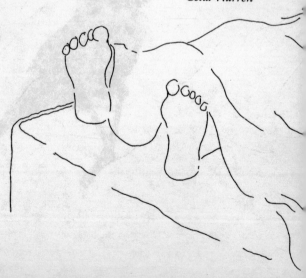

INDEX OF CONTRIBUTORS

Acknowledgements

The editor and publishers would like to thank the following for permission to use copyright material in this collection. The publishers have made every effort to contact the copyright holders but there are a few cases where it has not been possible to do so. We would be grateful to hear from anyone who can enable us to contact them so that the omission can be corrected at the first opportunity.

Andrew Abbott for 'Frogs in Water', by permission of *Cadbury's National Exhibition of Children's Art - Poetry Section*. Appeared in *The Best of Children's Poetry* ed. Jennifer Curry, pub. Red Fox, 1992.

Margaret Banthorpe for 'The Howl', first published in the magazine *Doors*, copyright the poet.

John Cotton for 'In the Kitchen' and 'Listen', from *Two by Two* (with Fred Sedgwick) pub. the John Daniel Daniel John Press, Ipswich, 1995.

Ellen Coffey for 'Underground Train' from *Wondercrump Poetry, 1994*, pub. Red Fox, 1995.

Pie Corbett for 'A Poem to be Spoken Silently', 'Summer Haiku' and 'Trying to Sleep', copyright the poet.

Jenny Craig for 'Autumn', copyright Jennifer Curry.

Jennifer Curry for 'Spring', copyright the poet.

Colum Deery for 'I Speak I Say I Talk'.

Berlie Doherty for 'I Hear...', first published in *School's Out!* ed. John Foster, pub. Oxford University Press, 1988, copyright the poet.

Gina Douthwaite for 'A Crack Band', copyright the poet.

John Foster for 'My Mum', copyright the poet and 'The Snow Monster', first published in *Monster Poems* by John Foster and Korky Paul, pub. Oxford University Press, 1995.

Katherine Gallagher for 'Rainstorm', copyright the poet.

Elizabeth Ingate of Debenham High School, Suffolk, for 'Chemistry Lesson'.

Mike Jubb for 'Unrattled' and 'Improved Reception', copyright the poet.

Lauren Julian for 'Body Sounds', first published in the *Thanet Anthology of Children's Poetry and Art*, 1987.

John Kitching for 'The Sound of Silence', copyright the poet.

Marcus Knight for 'Heavy Metal', by permission of *Cadbury's National Exhibition of Children's Art - Poetry Section*. Appeared in *The Best of Children's Poetry* ed. Jennifer Curry, pub. Red Fox, 1992.

Simon Laslett for 'The Concert', from *Imagine, An Anthology of Kent Children's Poetry*, by Kent Reading and Language Development Centre, 1987.

Karlen Lawrence for 'Bird (Play) Time', copyright the poet.

Gerda Mayer for 'Fragment' from *The Knockabout Show* by Gerda Mayer, copyright the poet.

Wes Magee for 'Noisy (and Quiet) Places', copyright the poet.

Tony Mitton for 'Rickety Train Ride' and 'The Reason Why', copyright the poet.

Brian Moses for 'Sounds' from *Hippopotamus Dancing*, published by Cambridge University Press, 1994 and 'The Cars that Leave Our Street', copyright the poet.

Gareth Owen for 'Cousin Janice with the Big Voice' from *My Granny's a Sumo Wrestler*, pub. Young Lions, 1994.

Brian Patten for 'The Whale's Hymn', from *Gargling with Jelly* by Brian Patten, pub. Viking Kestrel.

Emma Payne for 'A Quiet Life', copyright the poet.

Tim Pointon for 'The Sound of Tears', copyright the poet.

David Poulter for 'Music', copyright the poet.

Janis Priestley for 'Daybreak', copyright the poet.

John Rice for 'Noises off', copyright the poet.

Zoe Roscoe for 'The Red Bus Chugs', from *On Common Ground* by Jill Pirrie, pub. Hodder and Stoughton.

Oka Russell of Debenham High School, Suffolk, for 'Concerts'.

Emma Ripper of Debenham High School, Suffolk, for 'Children in the Park'.

Daphne Schiller for 'Manor House at Dusk', copyright the poet.

David Scott for 'Sort Of', from *How Does It Feel?* pub. Blackie.

Peter Sheton for 'Singing'.

Jennie Sinclair for 'Winter', copyright Jennifer Curry.

Ian Souter for 'Sounds Like', first published in *Poetry* by Ian Souter, pub. Scholastic, copyright the poet.

Robert Sparrow for 'In Class' and 'Having My Ears Done', copyright the poet.

David Thake Stallibrass for 'The Night Dad Turned 40!', copyright the poet.

Dave Ward for 'There Were These Two Girls' from *Candy and Jazzz* by Dave Ward, pub. Oxford University Press, 1994.

Celia Warren for 'Your Snores', copyright the poet.

Jane Whittle for 'Fast Rider' and 'Low Flying', copyright the poet.

Pauline Stewart for 'Birdsong Lullaby' from *Singing Down The Breadfruit*, pub. The Bodley Head, 1993.